THE McSORLEY POEMS

THE McSORLEY POEMS

VOICES FROM
NEW YORK CITY'S OLDEST PUB

Geoffrey R. Bartholomew

A CHARLTON STREET PRESS BOOK
NEW YORK

ACKNOWLEDGMENTS

The author wishes to thank the Matthew Maher family, proprietors of McSorley's Old Ale House, for their intelligence, encouragement, and good humor. Their support has helped immeasurably.

The author is exceedingly grateful to Bill Wander, McSorley historian, for the historical facts concerning the McSorley family.

The author owes a large debt of gratitude to Lila Gault and Robin Sunde for their support and friendship in the production of this book.

The author also wishes to thank Bob Hershon for his editorial assistance in the publication of *The McSorley Poems*.

*****

All the characters appearing in these poems are entirely fabricated from the author's imagination, as are the happenings within the poems.

*****

Copyright © 2001 by Geoffrey R. Bartholomew

ALL RIGHTS RESERVED. NO PART OF THIS BOOK MAY BE REPRODUCED OR TRANSMITTED IN ANY FORM OR BY ANY MEANS, ELECTRONIC OR MECHANICAL, INCLUDING RECORDING, PHOTOCOPY, OR ANY INFORMATION STORAGE AND RETRIEVAL SYSTEMS NOW KNOWN OR TO BE INVENTED WITHOUT PERMISSION IN WRITING FROM THE PUBLISHER, EXCEPT BY A REVIEWER, WHO MAY QUOTE BRIEF PASSAGES IN A REVIEW. FOR INFORMATION, WRITE THE CHARLTON STREET PRESS, 112 CHARLTON STREET, NEW YORK, N.Y. 10014. WEB ADDRESS: www.charltonstreetpress.com.

*****

FIRST EDITION

BOOK DESIGN: ELAN and JONATHAN BOGARIN

LIBRARY OF CONGRESS CONROL NUMBER: 00 - 133329

ISBN 0-9701325-2-2

Printed in the United States of America

CONTENTS

IF WALLS COULD SPEAK

The Wishbones	11
Il Bambino: Babe Ruth	12
Wall Haiku I	13
JFK Laughing	14
Polly & The Nude	16
Wall Haiku II	18
Birth of the Jackelope	19
Eavesdropping On Houdini's Handcuffs	20
Ceiling Haiku	21
Andersonville Shackles	22
On The Stump	23
Wall Haiku III	25
Lunch Respite	26
Wall Haiku IV	27
The Silence of Thumbs	28

UNSORTED REGULARS, MISFITS, LIARS HEROES & PSYCHOS

Frank O'Shaugnessy	31
Misyck, The Night Watchman	34
Doc Zory	36
Customer Haiku	39
Author In McSorley's circa 1970	40
Cyclops The Sniper	41
Dan Lynch	42
Kelly's Generation	44
Feduh The Immigrant	45
Deiter The Juiceman	47
Duggan The Drifter	48
Rectum Lips	50
Babushka From Chernobyl	51
Minnie The Cat	53
Kevin The Mad Stroker	55
Mad Deegan	56

Judith	58
Zepp	59
Glenn	61
Schmitty	62
Bogdan The Drunk	63
Timmy Boyle	64
Ben	66
The Life of Jimmy Fats	68
Bolles	72
Otto	74
Smiley	76

McSORLEY PHANTASMA

John McSorley	81
Annie McSorley	88
Peter McSorley	91
Kate	93
Delia (a.k.a. Mary) McSorley	94
James McSorley	96
Bill McSorley	97
Sarah McSorley	101
John McSorley	103
Kitty McSorley	104
John J. McSorley	106
Katherine Loretta McSorley	107
Edward McSorley	108
George McSorley	109
Jennie McSorley	110

FOR

My Beloved Patricia and Rafe

IF WALLS COULD SPEAK

THE WISHBONES

(A row of wishbones, covered with a century's dust, hangs over the old gaslamps at McSorley's Old Ale House.)

I.

Flesh we wore so long ago
trenchered by men of McSorley's
in the backroom below the mantle
roasted on the hob nigh years ninety
when the century was dewy with hope
hanging relics of nobody's men
sandhogs and soldiers galore
talk of buried cock and balled syph
joy of child and woman love
drudge of job and heat of ale
blood anger and sotten fists
years of talk garbled and forgotten
these single bones of birdbreast
flesh we wore long gone
dust upon dust the clacking die

II.

One story of men and their dust
McSorley regulars hung wishbones
      across the gas lampline
WWI bullshit, bad gas and bloodmud
those you see belong to the dead

III.

Ghost John says the bone truth
      is Catholic sacrament
Himself and Peter Cooper held
Bible House meetings right there
      round the big table
      turkey and ale
      beneath the fat nude
      mouths chumbling prayer
Louie Sawdust hung the wishbone
      mornings after
godspeed to all ghosts

IL BAMBINO: BABE RUTH

(Nat Fein's 1948 Pulitzer Prize photograph of the dying Babe Ruth, bidding farewell to all at Yankee Stadium, hangs over the original ale pumps at McSorley's.)

This is a good place
    to stop and rest
where so many have come
it is right for me
    to gaze from here
above the old ale pumps
sun off the shining brass
    in early afternoons
same glare as at the plate
this is a good home

Millions of eyes upon me
    upon these spindly limbs
this is not how it ends
Saturday nights I hear them
    surrounded by history
I hear them wondering
about me and my time
    what it must have been like
a patient Babe in the howling crowd
waiting for the pitch

The roar of roaring throngs
seamed orb descending home
    laughter and hope
oh, fickle god of shows
who gave me great days
who gave me this exit
    goodbye to all Yankees
the whole damn crowd fused
into this cancerous lump

WALL HAIKU I

THE GENERAL SLOCUM
(On June 15, 1904 the side-wheel steamer caught fire in the East River; 1,021 souls, mostly women and children from the St. Mark's German Lutheran Church on E. 6th Street, perished. They were on their way to a church picnic.)

Moms in picnic pose
Greed in rotted life jackets
Choking screams under

GUADALCANAL MOUSE
(A very small photograph of Ben Fay, former Marine and NYC fireman, and Joe Thornton, a.k.a. Joe Spuds, shows the two men at a table playing with a mouse.)

Joe escaped famine
Ben shot twelve Japs to save us
A mouse in a maze

McKINLEY'S SILENT TRIBUTE ON BROADWAY 1901
(A photograph depicts the New York multitudes—on Broadway & Wall Street—during the 5-minute national "Silent Tribute" to the slain President. It hangs on the west wall in the bar's front room.)

Gold my corpse gone cold
Trinity's spire fingers God
The mob weeps for me

JUNE 22, 1815 LONDON TIMES
(One of the oldest artifacts in the bar, the London Times announces the imminent military engagement in the lower right paragraph.)

Waterloo a blurb
Wellington meets you know who
Old news on the wall

JFK LAUGHING

(A bust of JFK sits atop the backbar above the old ale pumps.)

I was here once
right after the war
mostly old men then
I remember thinking this bar
      should be in Boston
      this smell is ours
my father's kind of joint
no rules on the wall but
      Be Good or Be Gone

The past a silent mummery
regular joes at elbows with
      the famous
      the moneyed
      the laborers
      the artists
      the students
the tourists gape and gawk
their callow askings indulged

The questions they utter:
—Was Kennedy here?
—Is that the original Death
      Certificate?

Stuck beside my famed portrait
a large desiccated mushroom
      sepia and fan-shaped
      an apt shadow growth
—What's that thing next to Kennedy?
I laugh with the other ghosts
the barman bluntest:
      —Part of his brain
they grunt

they fall silent
they offer
—Really?
—No shit.

My bust overlooking the Babe
ale, fire, talk, laughter
our gifts are here
Christmas is best
        me wearing Santa's hat

POLLY & THE NUDE

(A large painting of a nude graces McSorley's back room, she and her parrot overseeing, as it were, the action. The painting is a copy of Courbet's *La Femme au Perroquet*, probably done by a Cooper Union student in the last quarter of the 19th Century.)

A copy of a Courbet
just shows to go ya
more men have seen me
        than the real thing
which I got right here
straight outta Brooklyn,
        dearies!

After I posed for this
imitating Courbet's broad
Jimmy, the student painter
        Cooper Union's star
he introduced me to old John
I did him up real royal
        pulled his old Irish plug
but the old bastard was full of it
        got me knockered up

I should of owned that joint
        me, a woman
I went back in that condition
        Don't know you, he said
old Mr. Cooper was there
        took pity on me
        in privy paid me
to go live an' forget
my son the McSorley bastard
        he did okay
ran the Steeplechase at Coney
        great wife an' six kids
cops, nurses an' teachers
that's the real story

So they come in the back room
      stare, gawk an' glance
      lewd lads of America
outlive 'em all, I will
a secret is a secret
yep! ain't life grand!

WALL HAIKU II

LINDBERGH COMMEMORATIVE PLATE

(A plate issued in commemoration of Lindbergh's famous 1927 Atlantic flight sits behind the bar at McSorley's.)

I flew the ocean
Fame swollen like the cold sea
They stole our baby

WANTED POSTER FOR LINCOLN'S ASSASSIN

(An original wanted poster for John Wilkes Booth can be seen on the wall behind the McSorley taps.)

Edwin played Hamlet
I drank and plotted the deed
His long head bowing

STUFFED FLUKE

(A huge trophy fluke hangs on the corner wall near the old pumps.)

Flatfish state record
Blackened by fathoming time
I was Neptune's pet

THE McSORLEY NINE

(On the east wall near the front window is an 1877 photograph of a baseball team: The McSorley Nine.)

Silk breeze on our skin
Mystery in boyish games
Never safe at home

BIRTH OF THE JACKELOPE

(A jackelope sits atop the McSorley backbar cabinet, next to Peter Cooper's chair.)

Once white was I
an innocent Jack
deep as the sandman
up desert sleeves
down brown gullies
in drifting dreams
blurry stonefast

Perverse antelope
in my sleep he came
animus incubus
he buggered me a name
in my head they grew
two buttons to be
by summer I was reborn
the jackelope lie you see

Sliver of lead here
blowing a lunghole
out which my life bled
above me the sandman
    stick in hand
speaking his death tongue

Gutted and stuffed
the sandman glued antlers
    atop my skull
creating his myth

Next to Cooper's chair
    I sit
glassy-eyed drunk
antlers pointing at stars
white fur gray with dust

About my existence
the sandmen joke

The antelope
was left to rot
god knows where

EAVESDROPPING ON HOUDINI'S HANDCUFFS

(A pair of early 20th Century handcuffs, belonging to Harry Houdini, hangs from the McSorley ceiling near the giant oak icebox. Another pair, more modern, is cuffed to the barrail. These are sometimes, beguilingly, referred to as Houdini's handcuffs.)

Houdini was here.
Those are his cuffs up there.
(Guy looks up.)
Fuckin' Houdini.
Yeah. He was here.

Tourist: Where are Houdini's handcuffs?
Barman: There and there. Take your pick.
Tourist: Which are the real ones?
Barman: Both of them.
Tourist: Really?

How'd they get on the railing?
Houdini cuffed himself, then
    escaped, leaving them for posterity.
What's that?
You know. Tourists.

Was he really here?
Yep. He left his Mom
    outside. On the barrel.
No women allowed.
Those were the days.

A mama's boy.
But very athletic.
A Jew.
An escape artist.
A magician.

Houdini was here.
Those are his cuffs down there.
(Guy looks down.)
Fuckin' Houdini.
Yeah. Got away again.

CEILING HAIKU

CEILING NUTS

(A pair of coconuts dangles from the ceiling, purportedly sent by a famous French painter to John McSorley in the 19th Century.)

Two coconuts hang
Gifts from Gaugin to big John
Musk scent of brown thigh

CRABCLAW

(A huge claw is suspended from the McSorley ceiling.)

Born Alaskan king
Caught by one Samuel Clemens
Stranger in the air

ANDERSONVILLE SHACKLES

(The shackles hang alongside a bullwhip behind the bar.)

An ale with big John
I was not steeled for madness
Rust color of blood

A MEDIEVAL MACE

(A mace is hung from the ceiling near Cooper's chair.)

Archaic vision
Above visored eyes this sight
Spikes piercing white skull

THE BULLWHIP

(The bullwhip is rumored to have come from a southern slave-owner, or an infamous pirate.)

Bits of back flesh torn
Slaves and sailors lashed bloody
Mouthing cotton seas

ANDERSONVILLE SHACKLES

(A pair of Civil War ankle irons hangs from the bar's ceiling. They were given to John McSorley by a survivor of the prison camp's horrors, an Irishman from the 48th Regiment. The latter had been called *l'Enfants Perdus* because the New Yorkers filling its ranks were from every nation in Europe.)

It took a piece of luck
then some *real* evil doin'
maybe not doin', 'cause
you had to look away, let
some die if you was to live
wear a dead man's clothes
eat roast dog, cat or rat
snakes an' bugs from the swamp
watch friends go mad
mumblin' or ravin'
don't matter rage or fear
gangrene or gunshot
infection or a beatin'
hope some shiny bauble
no man could afford

Some rebs liked death
the *seein'* an' *hearin'* of a man
dyin', almost as if each man
maybe was dyin' different
might miss somethin', I guess

That cruel reb guard
who killed so many of us
I beat him with those irons
over an' over till blood flew
I told John what I did
I'*ll hang 'em up there*, he said
McSorley was a good man
gave us vets food an' ale
we'd tell our tales true
no women to see us weep
yep, old John even put
our photograph to the wall
cripples out on a picnic

ON THE STUMP

(A lithograph by G.C. Bingham, entitled *Stump Speaking*, depicts an orator amidst a crowd of common people, amongst whom is Abraham Lincoln. A tarnished brass plate on the bottom of the frame is dedicated to John McSorley.)

I sit amongst these people
commoners of which I am one
they understand plain words
so learned men must speak simply
put yourself in that man's shoes
would you suffer slavehood?
this is my simple argument
what our mothers have advised
do unto others as common-sense
all are equal in these states

To earn their trust I have fought
the toughest men in towns
which usually means a bully
even bested I will have won
such sentiment earns respect

These things I have been
shopkeeper, mill manager
postman, railsplitter
surveyor, lawyer
legislator
Whig and Republican
Commander-in-Chief
President
husband and father

Little Willie died
Mary and I weep nightly

the grief has no words
there is no solace
in war, in peace
we must push on

These faces around me
all have suffered loss
through such pain
we know each other
to seek the high ground

WALL HAIKU III

OLD GLORY ON THE MOON 1969

Barren gray old man
Stars and stripes over cold rock
Shadow of machine

McSORLEY CHOWDER CLUB 1877

(A photograph of an annual picnic on North Brother Island is on the wall at the end of the bar. Numerous members of the extended McSorley family can be seen in this photograph.)

Serious souls here
Shades caught by a camera
Eyes that tether ours

WOODY GUTHRIE'S ALBUM COVER

Joe Hill got drunk here
City mountains steel canyons
This land is our land

McSORLEY EXTERIOR: FATHER & SON

(In the east front window there is a poignant photograph from 1903, in which Old John is walking away from his saloon. His son, Bill, leans in the doorway, watching him go.)

Hunched father smiling
Always a son's dream to leave
On the house bright sun

PETER COOPER'S CHAIR

(Peter Cooper, founder of nearby Cooper Union, was a close friend of John McSorley. After his death, McSorley retired his chair atop a tall cabinet behind the bar.)

Cooper's arse was here
Hatching for the public good
Thinking in a cave

LUNCH RESPITE

Friday at Lunchtime:

Onions, sawdust & ale
carved tables clotted
with burgers & fries
cheddar & mustard
humans hunched at the eat

Through the door Toilet
shuffles Frank the Slob
men and women in midbite
as the utterance flies
      from the stall:
           "Fuckin' Bitch!"
ears wax, mouths gape
minds wonder - what the -
when Frank sounds the grunt
"Ughhhhhhhhhhhhhh Fuckin' Bitch!
Fuckin' Bitch! Fuckin' Bitch!"

Minutes later
to howls & applause
he exits
arranging
his apron

WALL HAIKU IV

LUNCH BUGLE

(A McSorley chef in the 1950s & 60s blew a bugle to announce that lunch was ready to be served. It hangs above the old kitchen doorway.)

Life is ravenous
Beef an' spuds, cheese an' onions
Stampalia blew it

BLACK HOBNAIL BOOTS

(A boy's pair of old black boots, rumored to have been Joseph Kennedy's, but more likely belonging to George McSorley, John's last son.)

The boy always ran
No time to show a son love
Old John hung them up

DEAD CEILING FANS

No one remembers
Smoky air pushed here and there
One night we just died

ROCKAWAY BEACH

(There is a photograph of two women at the turn of the 20th Century on Rockaway Beach.)

Women in the sand
Sunlit love flirts in the eye
George dove to his death

THE SILENCE OF THUMBS

(The Men's Room in McSorley's not only contains the original urinals, but the door itself is unique. Many millions of thumbs have created a silky smooth crater beneath the door handle. There is now a tiny hole where the wood has been worn through.)

Whoever heard
of a shithouse door
with mullioned windows
hiding those huge urinals
yet she's there
promising relief
above the door it says:
        $2 Show

But *it* is also here
the silent sliding
of thumb over wood
in opening this door
a smooth hole in time
each man rubbing free
a molecule of wood

Leaving a tiny hole
in this greater fabric

Which with time
will grow larger
the door, most likely, will
disappear, and (thumbs
being what they are)
this will all begin again

UNSORTED
REGULARS, MISFITS, LIARS
HEROES & PSYCHOS

FRANK O'SHAUGNESSY

In some woods near Cologne
        in cold sunlight
as a good medic
I cradled what was left
of some G.I.'s head
when the bullet hit me
it ripped away some skull

They put a metal plate
inside my fuckin' head
a plump German nurse
blew me for a year
        except on Full Moons
I brought her home to Mom
on old East 7th Street

In the carpenter's union
I was a knockdown man
nights I got drunk at McSorley's
Marlena only blew me once
        leaving the door open
        so Mom would see
I beat her too much
she was screwing the brains
        out of some guy downstairs
she took the kids an' left
Mom said it was the plate
I don't know, maybe
kids never spoke to me again
I can still feel that wet hole
        my fingers
        inside the guy's head

In the bar I was The Slob
I'd sing my wild woman song

>   about wantin' a woman
>   that drinks, stinks, an' thinks
> I did the sawdust, the dishes
>   the onions, the shitter, too
> act dumb, play the drunk, sing
> somebody'd buy me an ale

Once, with my heavy hammer
I beat on the huge urinals
at the V.A. detox
I asked the doctors
           maybe it's the plate?
           was it rusting?

In a drunken rage one night
           I got Tourettes
           some cursin' disease
"Fuckin' Bitch! Fuckin' Bitch!"
           in mutters an' shouts
           in yawps an' yells
the union never called anymore
into the bar stormed wild women
it was gettin' late for me
           fuckin' bitch

Scummers made me a mule
like Joe Spuds the gofer
up an' down cellar steps
haulin' onions an' potatoes
           for a couple ales
near the end I got mixed up
fuckin' bitches everywhere
I couldn't wash the feel
           off my hands
           fuckin' bitch

Yeah, in the last days
I would bolt the chili
      then spew it in the stall
stomach shot, bad plate
ulcers, *fuckin' bitch*
then the old lady died
fucked me good, *fuckin' bitch*
in the wet hole, that's it
      with gettin' old
nothin' *fuckin'* works *bitch*

So January 22, 1991
      out in the cold sunlight
      down 7th Street
      I walked
where Max's Books & Records
      used to be
      my heart blew up
isn't that a *fuckin' bitch*...

MISYCK, THE NIGHT WATCHMAN

I sit alone here at night, listening
    doors and windows twisted
    by McSorley's heavy sag
    everything out of whack
    creak and groan of ghosts
    they speak, you know
    but Woodrow Wilson there
    I can't understand him
    he garbles his words

My brother Jerzy's dead thirty years tonight
    we grew up here on 7th Street
    St. George's, God and girls,
    stickball, cars and beer
    then we started the skag
    Jerzy shot up first
    I was belting my arm
    when he sat back
    his eyes went real wide
    like flooring the Buick
    feeling that crazy rush

Bill McSorley up there by the icebox
    resembles Teddy Roosevelt
    a smaller moustache
    timid eyes, sour mouth
    really did love his old man
    vowed to keep the bar *as is*
    kill time in this real place
    now just a face on the wall
    the bar a mute witness
    to Bill's doomed love

My favorite relic is the playbill from the 1880s
    a windmill and two dutchgirls
    on a forlorn spit of land
    the ocean a white-capped menace

What Are The Wild Waves Saying?
some March nights it blows
so hard against the windows
I'd swear it's Jerzy's voice

Larry, homeless black wraith, taps the window
    I make him a liverwurst on rye
    some nights he has d.t.s
    tonight he's soulful
    I fucked up, he says
    shoeless, he begins again
    his scabrous circle
    East Village Odysseus

The ripe nude in the painting back there
    I don't like her much
    she knows she's got it
    that mouth of plump disdain
    the parrot probably trained
    to do weird shit, yeah
    they liked that stuff back then

And on every wall this guy Peter Cooper
    rich and famous in 1860
    John McSorley's buddy
    they say he brought Lincoln here
    after some Great Hall speech
    that's real strange, me here
    where Lincoln once drank

At night I oil the old bar
    there's a sag in the middle
    the mahogany a wornout horse
    I know it's stupid, but I think
    Jerzy's going to appear one night
    we're all gonna sit here and talk
    him and Cooper and McSorley,
    Lincoln, Woodrow Wilson,
    maybe the fat nude, too

DOC ZORY

Big Z was my old man
first Gypsy violinist
       to play Carnegie Hall
Ma died young on us
so he taught me the axe
honing an edge to call shadows
until beauty was airborne
I'd hear him at wolf's hour
       that moan of catgut
       barely touching
then madly bowing
wrenching their love
when he died
I joined the Navy

Battleship South Dakota
monikered the *Shittydick*
       Japs kamikazeed us
from wide steel decks
my friends a bloody jigsaw
I hosed heads, torsos & legs
at night I played the axe
       as us boys wept
those were the days

Carl, Johnny Purple & me
we played the Havana cruises
pussy, booze, gambling
the 50s blew a Gypsy's dream
       then Castro came
Superman, huge Cuban cockman
butchered like a side of beef
       dictators & big shots
       no sense of humor

McSorley's was New York
home to every shade
    ukies, polacks,
    guineas & micks
    flatheads, fags
    niggers & spics
    kikes, wasps
    wankers & wops
you name 'em they're drinking
gigs playing here & there
upstairs in the still summer heat
the boys humped their whores
while I bowed my axe

Then the Panther leaped
    these Gypsy bones
me loving a guinea woman
the old man must've spit worms
god, how I loved her
    cancer took her at 44
    she wasted in my arms
for two years I couldn't play

Our son studied the knife
became a heart surgeon
with hands of these hands
he cuts to Beethoven's D Major
there's blood in the music

My last years a *scherzo*
in McSorley's dim cave
    I played the porter
swabbing the toilets
shit, piss & vomit
what hands of diamonds
    Heifetz, oh god!
no way to explain away

nags, whores & booze
these spiraling
gypsy genes

J.J. gave me Saturdays
      on the floor
a month later I was dead
the bath was so hot
I could feel my heart
      fluttering Paginini
I made it to the bed
then felt the bow drive
      toward some chord
deep in the Bumblebee
where Panther & Big Z wait

Down at cold Jarema's
amidst the flower stench
over my coffin
the gypsy men bowed
weeping axes

CUSTOMER HAIKU

(In 1909, Freud, Jung, Adler, and other psychologists from Europe were invited to lecture at Clark University in Worcester, Mass. In New York, they stopped at McSorley's after listening to a lecture in Cooper Union's Great Hall.)

FREUD

Dirty common men
White potbelly of hot coals
Lies to pump false pride

JUNG

Rhythm in the words
Sunblast lighting male profile
The soul in silence

ADLER

This pub a test-tube
Men act from fear, barman says
Inferior fate

BARMAN

Bearded professors
Unease among working men
Mind the word thinkers

OLD JOHN McSORLEY

Spittoon and horse gone
A thought hawkered in sawdust
Death in the shithouse

JOHN SLOAN

Barsketching of men
Paint the everyday noble
Eyes chasing the real

AUTHOR IN McSORLEY'S circa 1970

I.

In vast childhood time
always tomorrow to tell
here by the coalstove, long
before she was born
old men sucked cigars
to dream in smoke
spat gobbets of word
to bolster the deed
nursed ale for decades
where tales were fired
her father sat here

II.

Plainpretty, you know, she
sits alone at the start
a procession before her
coalfire heat curling a plot
jotting down the ideas
a book for the wormfarm
the drunk's dustjacket framed
idea and dream in cracker grist
in just such sawdust design
she will speak her truths

CYCLOPS THE SNIPER

In McSorley's 1972
a blustery gray Paddy's Day
some asshole clubbed me
down in the brawl I went
sawdust, blood and shards
damn shillelagh knob
took the right eye

In Nam I was a sniper
now they call me Cyclops
strange, but before the fight
      in the shithouse stall
this broad named Dawn
      got hold of the hilt
      like it was a mike
announcing, Well, Well,
If it isn't the One-Eyed Beast

I still drink in McSorley's
everybody's gone now 'cept Bart
he was there, he remembers
now I wash the fucking windows
in all the Mom & Pop joints
so people can see themselves

This gray marble in my cold
      fixed stare
no need to shave every day
some benefit package
but every fall I get my buck
at a couple hundred yards
this good eye works fine
I can still pop 'em quiet
right there in the heart

DAN LYNCH

Back in the old sod I taught
history, arcane Celtic secrets
no room for thought an' word
young an' brash an' liked my cups
at 30 I was in the Bronx
an apron made me a barman
whiskey an' quick fists
met your man, J.J., keen an' crafty
brought me down to McSorley's
students, workers, artists
not like the Bronx louts
met the India Pales, too
Ballantine's green saints
Blackburn the poet said I
sucked 'em like a baby a breast

I loved the Snowqueen
another man's wife
in whiskey oblivion
the lads put me in detox
sobered twice, I almost died
Marlboros an' coffee an'
old Mum's greasy fry
rashers oily pink in the sun
took the cure of meetings
Mum died alone one night
the kettle whistling away
took her back I did
to the Cork wormfarm

In black night hours
tea after sober tea
a fifty year old man
makes a jigsaw of it
a busted pipedream

Snowqueen's liver burst
an' we never touched

Lung pain came an' went
metastasized in my brain
I shrank to a rattle
my eyes beaming alone
from this gray pouch
faces came an' spoke
things I could not heed
I kept seeing Mum
cooking me a fry

KELLY'S GENERATION

Before I went off to war
my father took me here
      I knew the smell
      onions and ale
      sawdust and age
an Army Ranger I was
shipping out the next day
brash, proud and scared
he wanted to share his bar
shadows on grizzled men
Leiderkranz and cheddar
gnarled hands of labor
he knew I might die

I killed a lot of Germans
guys with wives and kids
mostly regular joes
killing regular guys
who had to be killed

I bring my son here
      to rub wood and elbow
      drink from heavy mugs
      to see in this light
faces that mirror
friend and ghost

what was unspeakable
still is
you never tell them how
you did what you did
because what you saw
still is

In winter afternoons
I hear us talking
around and around
talking softly

FEDUH THE IMMIGRANT

Feduh, they call me *Feduh*
from Ukraine I am
here in secretly
      no problem
work to send home moneys
      wife and children
I leave them for here
      Amerika, freedom
dishes I do at Ukeydiner
clothes work in laundry
labor in old McSorley
treat me good
      freedom no problem
laughs and moneys to eat
      hamburgers, fries
sawdust, cokes and beers
girljoke lots I speak
      English dirt words
poosee, kokk no problem

good heart Amerikanski
but make fun on me
to me they call *Feduh*
      great laughs
in McSorley *feduh* is
      ale slime I clean
      stuff under bar
I no care, joke for me
      no problem
is joke for all, too
to them I call *huiedupi*
in Ukraine dickass
all laugh big one joke
      feduh and *huiedupi*

but bad happen to Feduh
I not know this blowjob
on avenue I pay hookah
       on my kokk she hum
sounds of Ukey anthem
I dreaming of homeland
hit my face some man
       nose teeth crush
       now ache balls
       kokk leak
       freedom, disease
lots of pills, no money
I get cure, go home soon
       see family
Amerika, no problem

DEITER THE JUICEMAN

They called me Juiceman
with electrics I was the best
wire a house or an anus
melted gooks in Nam
sparks shot from all holes
coppered Alaskan pipe, too
I was the fucking Juiceman

My old man did this
made me, taught me
took me to 42nd Street
peeps and pornos
hated Mom he did
        probably as much
as I hate Lana
Mom went and hanged herself
Lana took my kid
        ran off with her dyke friend
I'll wire her up
        so her eyebrows glow blue

I ain't handsome
running to fat's the truth
I was wiring a/c at McSorley's
        when I met the garbageman
        black leather and chains
try anything once, so it
was back to his joint
        in a black Toronado
he tied me down bad
had his way with a dildo
then he slit me up the middle
when I was screaming
        he slashed my throat
my own blood got me
me, the fucking Juiceman

DUGGAN THE DRIFTER

I stayed two years behind the bar
longer than usual for me
this insane lust to move
town to town, woman to woman
bar to bar, jack of trades

I knew J.J. from the ship
himself, Mahoney, Lloyd an' me
self-exiles, hungry young men
whiskey, rumors of jobs an' love
hearsay the gossamer web
J.J. gave me work an' a promise

I was two years behind that bar
pumping ale to American lads
who had no idea nor need
        to roam this country
I thought of hunkering down again
the young waiter lad, Seamus,
he could have been my son

But I twitched the web
she found me fast she did
that wife of long ago
a hound for hate an' money
the kids she turned on me
J.J. said he had no choice
if I stayed he'd garnishee
        so I lit out again

Two years behind that old bar
mahogany touch silk like
        a young thing's breast
the ale bittersweet in your nose
        scent of my father
he could have been my son
that waiter lad, Seamus

J.J. gave me two weeks wages
toward Jackson Hole I drove
across America's blacktopped soul
to sell ice cream in the desert

RECTUM LIPS

It isn't my fault
    I'm fat and pasty
my misshapen head
    straw on a gourd
yes, it's men I like
their physical moves
    so supple
    so strong
I am gay, quietly so

On slow nights here
I let my eyes cruise
they come in groups
    three, four, five
    oblivious
to my twitching lips

There are times I stand
    at the urinal
    schlong in hand
    watching the men
    do their business
once in a while someone
    will threaten
to put my head through the wall
    I get scared
    harder, too

The bartenders suffer me
    as a character
behind my back I'm R.L.
    Rectum Lips
which isn't apt since
    like the *kosinski* guy
I just like to watch

BABUSHKA FROM CHERNOBYL

Annya, from Chernobyl I am
there I sell the vegetables
an old fat woman
babushka grandma
my family grow blisters
forty in all we are
the potatoes look good
        no black pocks
in Kiev to visit Vasyl
I took him beauties

The clouds blow alarms
wind and sirens stitch air
roads crowd so I walk home
        all night in screams
        trucks redcross crawl
two nights to the village
my family grow blisters
        my little grandchildren
my sons and daughters
like potatoes they rot
seven die on fourth day
ten on fifth, ten on sixth
two on seventh day, then me
        I live
in Kiev Vasyl buys ticket
finish life with cousins
later I come, he says
I know he no coming

In America on 7th Street
I sweep walks for McSorley's
Sunday mornings I mop halls
        drunk Irish in shorts
        hand on his kielbasa

    other hand wave dollars
Babushka is old and smelly
    she cannot do sex things
with mop I hit him
I need alone in halls
   to mop and weep
the blisters grow black
   then burst rotten
I am old and fat Ukrainian
behind my back I hear them
saying me, Babushka,
is contaminated
   yes, with pocks
   and black weeps

MINNIE THE CAT

I.   Lazing About

My O my, it's me
Minnie
Minnie the cat
my grayness a presence
my lazy lope through sawdust
around shoes & over butts
this fallen saltine here
chunk of cheddar there
what I'm looking for
         when I'm not looking for
         that fucking fast mouse
is a free chair by the stove
curl up behind the heat
listen to the coal hum
dream of caterwaul lust
         mice murmur in the wall
         a kitten making pie
my grayness a presence
loping through decades

II.   Stalking

It came out of the shitter
a lightblind zigzag waterbug
crunchy & big as my hindpaw
         teeth itch
         whiskers tighten
he darts stops darts
         crawls on some guy's cuff
I'm still ten feet from leap
now he's moving up the pantleg
I'm closer, lower, lower
         he's on the guy's thigh

I'm flying eyes zooming
        my claws digging into meat
the crunchy fucker's mouthed
now the table's overturned
chili & mugshards in the sawdust
hubbahubba the boys are pissed
a few crunches & it's over
I love the skittering legs
        in my mouth

KEVIN THE MAD STROKER

I loved 'em, loved 'em all!
I didn't care none 'bout looks
that's for the rich boys
the magazine wankers
no, it's the funlovers for me
the laughers, the skinny
the ugly, plain, or pretty
the hefty an' the shy, we'd do it
do it, an' do it again!
BeJesus! Take me Bridget!

Three years in the alehouse
workin' an' livin' upstairs
three years of lovin' women
smart or dumb, wild or scared
I loved 'em an' they me
so Sean left, said I was dirty
tired of cleanin' up an' all
wasn't much fun after that
I loved my brother Sean

Then I got sick
the new plague
me, the Irish stallion
I had these scabs
      the size of sugarbeets
swarmin' over my body
me, lover of all girls
this from all my lovebugs
three months I was dyin'
my corpse stank up the hall
Sean, my own blood
      disowned me
so they laid me down
in this field called Potters

MAD DEEGAN

On the bustling sidewalk
as the last gray light slides
      between concrete walls
I move brokenly, madness
a hunched raven on my shoulder
behind Dean & DeLuca's glass
the elegant consume
      and defecate elsewhere
invisible yet ubiquitous
I shit on dark corners
urinate with the feral
apologia to Lowry
      but I am his pariah dog
      still alive in the ravine
howling, quietly howling

Educated with the elite
Stuyvesant then Yale
in the Seminary I became
      a brother of inculcation
so I taught God's children
the nun Betty and I
      fell in love's despair
we quit our vows to marry
      we ate acid
quickly madness won us over
with fists we fought
our words weapons of delight

Betty took a train to
      somewhere, leaving then
this tunnel in my brain
a small black smudge
with their pills the shrinks
      would me heal a hole

At McSorley's I swept up
for simple cash and food
washed pots and pans despite
the burgeoning smear
    which one night
blotted the running bullshit
        leaving the mind a nub
        where the raven pecks
I am searching the streets
catching the last sliding light
    on my hunched form
the pariah dog is here
    is here somewhere

JUDITH

Alone in McSorley's
        fingers across old oak
        carved names
        in dead time
I sit reading his letter
my lover proposes from afar
        across the street
        kids chase a mongrel
written words about *forever*
I pile sawdust with my shoe
        dead trees
the second ale buzzes warmth
        my head hale and thick
sunlight shot through glass

A derelict pushes saloon doors
        as the bartender barks
        the bum fingers the world
how he cannot live without me
        beyond the cat's cliché
my fingers across his chest
touch in the afternoon heat
as in this moment seized
a woman alone with an ale
        gold light of New York
        loveletters and children
        homeless mongrels
eddy of reflection to choose
here comes my cheddar platter
        onions and crackers
me at this windowtable
having a moment of my life

ZEPP

I did a liddle a dis
    a liddle a dat
dis is da way I speak
I grew up on da block
right here on Seven an' Toid
we useda push da swingin' doors
    yell at old John Smit
    vaffuncculo
    upyourmudder
shit like dat
da whole block smelled ale

Hall Place was da Ale Place
Gypsy Bolles came out at night
    climb da ladder an' paint
    change da fuckin' sign
dere was a barber shop
    suckers an' bags a hair
    set 'em afire for da Ukeys
hated dat 'cause of da war
Nazi shit smells like dat

My old man drank in dere
end a da bar he used ta stand
him an' da Silvey brudders
    truckin' da toxic shit
    every Friday night in dere
Mom'd send me to bring 'em back
big fuckin' fight every time
den my old man got da cancer
    ate his bowel like da worm
    had dat shitbag on da hip
    still went in dere, too

Got drunk wid da boys dat Friday
    gave me da kisses dat night

                when I came ta fetch 'em
Silvey brudders drove 'em out dere
        ta da Brooklyn Bridge
        dey said he swandived

I drive da trucks now
        some Friday nights I go in dere
in McSorley's in da July heat
        da smell is same as ever
I drink an' tink of my old man

GLENN

I had some genius
I did
DeNiro & me, when we were kids
we did shit
drinking, fighting
I had ideas, too

I drove the cab for cash
when I picked him up
we talked old times
I got a screenplay
he gave me his card
        send it, I'll have a look
I did
first, I heard nothing
then I sent a card
I got a note back
        thanks, it's not for me
        keep writing
        see you around
            Bobby

The guy who stabbed me
even looked like him
a lousy five dollar fare
I should've let it go
right in the spleen
I could feel the leak
all the way to Bellevue
on the stretcher
lying there in the hallway
I wondered if it might help
to tell them I knew Bobby

SCHMITTY

In this old bar
I've come for years
to watch for love

No matter the insults
I never took them to heart
Shitty Schmitty
faggot, queer, queen
fudgepacker
shirtlifter
yes, one of those
I was always like that
born that way
Mother was tough
the old man dead
into advertising
I wrote copy
dreaming of *you*
I sold you soap
cars and razors
gadgets and gizmos
I sold you *her* smile
her glistening lips
you fantasized
buying illusions
paying one way
while I was the other
'round and 'round
like a carousel
for cash or pleasure
the old in & out

In this old bar
I've come for years
to watch for love
believe me,
it's not here

BOGDAN THE DRUNK

I know it why
I am big drunk
I fight the Nam gooks
I lose many friends
I see them bleed on me
I drink to forget
I drink to remember
I lose my hope
I see my mother die
I see father die
I know it why
I am big drunk
I have my room
I know my girlfriend
I know she leaves me
I know it why
I have swollen liver
I do not care
I have freedom
I come to McSorley's
I drink of light and dark
I am to explode spleen
I am cursed by leeches
I see men think
I see men fight
I see enough
I am big witness
I see too much
I am big drunk
I know it why

TIMMY BOYLE

Me, Timmy Boyle!
up there with Babe Ruth
Lincoln's Wanted Poster
an' Robert Emmet, too

—What a painting! they say
         pointin' above the taps
—He really caught McSorley's!
—Check out that bartender!
—Perfect! You can see his feelings!
—And he got the sunlight, too!
—Check out the guys at the bar!
—It's every ginmill that ever was!

Me, Timmy Boyle!
barman for a day
fillin' in for Lynch
I remember the painter
         sketched a bit
         took snapshots
the daffy woman in the sailorsuit
         drank off her porters
         then beckoned me over
—Tenspot, suck your cock in the hall?
Sweet Jesus,
         I did nothin' but stare
—Faggot! said she an' walked out
the two of us wed forever
estranged inside that paint

Frank the slob
         his back to the world
Bart says he was special
the other guy a Korean War vet

doin' time in Singsing
> manslaughter
> ran over some kids
> a mean drunk

That belly is my liver
wife says the kids hate me
but look at that!
I'm up there forever:
Me, Timmy Boyle!

BEN

The day before I joined up
this was June of '43
the old man took me to this joint
dark like some old cave
old geezers nursing ale
workers leaning on the bar
sawdust, sputum and sweat
a realm of men and mantalk
at eighteen it was *mystery*

My old man pointed there
on the wall: *The McSorley Nine*
There's only eight, I said
that smile, a slow nod
I didn't get it then
the barman, John Smith
      wished me Godspeed
men were dying

On Guadalcanal
      and other nameless
islands, I stitched with lead
a lot of Japanese, enough
for a couple baseball teams
      that's the way
      it was played

Standing here at the bar
fifty odd years later
a young Japanese couple
asks me to take a snapshot
I direct them on either side
of the McSorley Nine
I ask him what his father did
      in WWII

he die, he says with solemnity
I nod with respect
his wife wants to know why
only eight men in the old photo
It's a *mystery,* I say

THE LIFE OF JIMMY FATS

Call me Jimmy
I'm not fat, I'm obese
nowhere to hide, pal
but I learned something
people love you
        if you're real fat
I mean, really huge
you save them

So I got my first job
        in Coccia's on 7th Street
        Italian sit-down deli
Jewish actors from Second Avenue
Ukey Moms from the block
laborers, clerks from Wannamaker's
number-runners an' schoolkids
        you know the years
        how they quietly roar by
I was the best short-order guy
        ate like a champ
then Artie sold the building

Two doors up was the saloon
busy lunch an' lazy afternoons
nights packed with young guys
J.J. the owner knew me from when
I was a kid, burned my arm on
his '48 Buick, Irish guys laughing
that fat kid in the photo, that's
me, walking by the bar in 1950

Stampalia the chef had just died
        announcing lunch
        he'd sound an old bugle
        this time his aorta blew

I got the job
old guys in the bar whispered
but I was big, fast, an' funny
no bugles, just Jimmy Fats
I won 'em over with laughs
I loved that place

In the doo-wop band
        I sang lead, us guys
        from Aviation High
we cut some songs, never made it
Joey overdosed on skag
Lou got married with kids
Willy stepped on a mine in Nam
me, I kept cooking an' eating

McSorley's in the 70s
        me an' Frank the Slob
        we humped it all
Ray the waiter, then George
        he was the best
        took care of everyone
workers, cops, students, firemen
we played nags an' numbers
        then George quit
        oldtimers died off
Frank's fuckin' bitch drone began
waiters coming an' going
        the only sane ones
Minnie the cat an' me

Shit, I was up to 630 by '79
when I fell in love
Lace was beautiful and big
so we starved an' screwed to 260
after the baby, she got mental
nights she cried a lot

it sounded like me far off
but I can't remember when

One black night I woke up
      Lace was gone
note said she went to L.A.
      that was it
I don't think it was love
just some kind of lonely thing
      fat people get

Still, I was McSorley's chef
I was 500 an' floating
      little Tanya screaming
      Daddy! Daddy! Daddy!
raising a kid alone ain't easy
the fucking dog Blacky
      big Lab, shedding
hated the heat he always did
I was on the throne when he
ripped her head halfway off
      broke her neck
the funeral was like Ma's
at Lancia's on Second Avenue
next to the old 21 Place
the guys from the bar
murmured condolences
      shook their heads
if Lacey hadn't run away
if I hadn't been on the shitter
if, if, a million *ifs*

Back at work
Frank's *fuckin' bitch*
      became a foul mantra
nothing to say nor do
that's when I began

        to eat
really eat

I couldn't get out of bed
fucking buzz in my ear
      a numb hissing
        finally I got up
then the buzz was a hornet
the floor rose up, stung me
sideways the last thing I saw
some pizza crust and the doll
Tanya's dusty Barbie

That was the end of Jimmy Fats
they buried me out in Queens
      between Tanya an' Ma
the stone says 1939-1990
but how's anybody to know
      you know
what *really* happened?

BOLLES

(Bob Bolles was a Village character in the '60s, '70s, and '80s, a painter and iron sculptor who played and worked hard; a throwback to an earlier time, he supported himself as a jack-of-all-trades. He died of cirrhosis in 1988.)

Doing what I want to do
red bandanna round my head
imp grin in a sweaty face
wispy moustache
hands greased on black jeans
dirty denim workshirt
shitkicking boots, yeah
I'm the real Village
hipflask of Jack Daniels
I'm the Gypsy Artist
doing what I want to do

In McSorley's we sat & drank
painters & poets & drunks
just like in Queens growing up
they all made fun of me
thought I was a *manqué*
yet I fucked their women
the world hates a little guy

By '70 they were famous or dead
so one night I made it my table
I moved in above the bar
became the super & star
Sundays we cleaned the joint
my crew of young studs
work for ale & a few bucks
they thought I was hotshit
acetylene rig out back
torches & steel a blueburn
to twist the curves of lust

Ballsass naked I cooked
shrimp, ginger & scallions
round & round in the big wok
Jan sucked me while I stirred
Gail I did with her 3 year old
riding shotgun round my neck
the big-titted Austrian babe
a thunderclap fart when she came
me mirrored above, watching
the frenzy from atop my torch
I sculpted them as I fucked
their legs & tits adangle
oh, I was great then I was
doing what I want to do

In Soho's early years
Broome Street was mecca
I caroused, made my art
drank old Jack D. the while
'til the booze blurred my brain
balls the size of grapefruits
now I couldn't leave bed
without my silver flask
doing what I want to do
at St. Vincent's they didn't get it
me, Bolles, the Gypsy Artist
so my liver burst
I howled at the end
a torch firing my myth

Now in McSorley's
atop the backbar I rest
next to opium pipes,
cop badges & bullets
aside Kennedy's head
along with Sullivan's fists
I sit in my silver flask
all ashes and a bit of bone

OTTO

(Arthur Arnold, a.k.a. Otto, lived on East 7th Street for half a century. He worked in McSorley's as a chef, and later as a porter.)

My name is Otto the German
though I hated my landsmen
I understood their murdering
that sliver of perfection
                              stuck
in the visor of childhood
the child stepping on the bug
a perfect fear atop the sole

With my uncle I came to America
a butcher in the meat market
he raised me as a shadow
took me to the old bar where
I watched men talk and drink
                              laugh
at their puny dreams of love
here, the ale in their maws
they could admit attrition
a sheep's tumorous tripe
their minds riddled like that
I listened closely enough

I could not play in romance
for a butcher sees red innards
love was for the imperfect
I adored thick chops and spuds
only one woman for me
Gert, her breasts and thighs
we loved to Mozart at night
when she got sick
they took off her breasts

I didn't care
she died anyway
our baby with her

In McSorley's I sat in old age
days and nights shaded to one
years were smoke from a cigar
while young men came to me
asking for an old man's wisdom
—What's it all mean, Otto?
I hawk the gray mucus gobbet
rap the cane on the floor
—Bullshit, my black utterance

SMILEY

I'm old with ten teeth
arthritis grips me
my memory's shiteshot
an invisible seine
      drawing me in
nothing to do but smile

In the bar with the boys
that's home now, that smell
      onions, sweat an' ale
I love pushing through them
      swinging saloon doors
everyman gets his entrance
over an' over again

I smile teeth for the boys
      get them laughing
propping up my twisted hand
my two fingered claw
      signalling for a pair
I used to pitch in the Twenties
      the Brooklyn Seagulls
life is knowing the seams
      how to grip a fastball

I ask old Tom, how's the wife
      bedridden by a stroke
      hanging in there
      he says, real slowly
staring through his ale
this being the sole hour
      he leaves her each day
some days he talks shop
      when down a manhole
      a perp actually fled

           into stench an' black float
           fuck 'em, Tom said
           me an' my partner we
           just slid back the manhole
I like talking with Tom
he's seen some things

Once, while I was pissing
           a young woman opened the door
           she stared at me
           sorry, she said
           you look like my father
when I came out she was gone

So we talk some politics
           lots of sports
sometimes joke about the girls
I don't say much, just smile
sort of sad, us boys blew it
there's this ache
           as if something went by
no name to it
not even sure we'd have known it

I wanted to tell that woman
           the daughter I had
           who died of the blood
some kind of leukemia
now I wake up with her face
           in the dream
I can't get myself zipped
           fast enough
if I ever see her again
I'd do something about my teeth
tell her something special

Come winter, Tom an' I
we sit by the potbelly
      talk of guys long gone
      jobs an' kids an' aches
watch Bart shake her down
      throw on some coal
      bank her for the heat
J.J. comes in, buys a round
plays boss, sniping an' bitching
I wonder if he knows
      how great this joint is

McSORLEY PHANTASMA

JOHN McSORLEY

(b.1827, d. 1910. He opened "The Old House At Home" in 1854; the bar's name was changed to "McSorley's Old Ale House" after his death.)

I.   1911   In Waiting Now

Hurly-burly of ale an' flesh
young lads out a gashing
chancres an' pus the price to pay
ah, good men I knew to drink
       as pox sucked their brains
strayed I did, love's milk sweet
a habit it was, so I sought
       Mr. Cooper's counsel
weekly we supped an' quaffed at
       the hob table here
politics, help the working soul
but said I, astutter, cursed I be,
       A wwwwwoman had her wwwwway
wwwwwith me, wwwwwhat's to do?
Not to worry, famous Cooper winked
A busy thumb an' slack red meat
       for lips will God pardon
then his skeletal cackle rose, so
       laughed I with him
men of same sin, different station
I daren't tell him it was Kitty
       she was but the housegirl
nursemaid to my dying wife Annie
shame stains even a ghost

But dead now so I am, so whence
the ghosts of my loved ones?
here I wait for them, my wives
the fallen and broken children
here I wait their passing shades

we must speak before leaving
    this limbo

II.   1919   Wishbones

No luck for some of our lads
so their bones shall gather dust
don't let anyone forget them
when the curious ask, tell them
those bones belong to the dead
good boys an' men killed in war
let their dust go to dust
as we living bear witness

III.   1929   Yours, My Son

The pub's yours, my son, all yours
of course, Kitty mistrusted ye
not her blood yours, but Annie's
'tis true, she put it in the will
let himself wait till we are gone
fearful for Jennie, she was
what ye might do to the poor girl

IV.   1939   Wingless

There's nought here methinks
    baubles to tary the mind
    the mobs unaware as sheep
promise of youth in gold afternoon
the poor are poor are still poor
wretches an' wraiths dying slowly
laughter in the human din
dark mahogany an' strong ale
as words men mince an' mumble
while I wait for *their* voices

Chumble, chatter an' splatter
what breed of cretin gods

us men, wingless, picking
    at old cheese
    raw onions
    no ladies

Now Jennie wanders the halls
Creedmore her house at home
a mad waif forever
the spitting image of Kitty
O, dumb beauty of genes
hers or mine twisted
I no longer need know

Often, on black eves
    before streets went lamplit
I wondered where she went
to some life in Brooklyn
if she thought of me
while she humped her man
    there is too much light
on her naked beauty here
I am the invisible parrot
if ghosts were to drown
abloat with grief I'd be
I wish a ghost would pass

V.   1949 A Wait for Wives

Annie thought me nought
but foul an' coarse, catering
to that smelly mix of men
she failed to see beyond the bar
men's need to talk an' plot
laugh an' suffer one another
o'er a few pints at play
yet she bore me children

an' though they fled in ways
their own, an' death, too
I did love her, I did

Those first years were best
on hot nights our bodies
       danced on the wall
       candlelit shadows
the horsehooves clopped away
there was no end to bounty
Peter an' Delia born
       before the worm turned
then little James born an' died
little John come an' gone the same
her rage at God sullied her inners
till that terrible thing grew within
       how was I to know
when I hired the young Kitty

Never the same after Jennie
       no feeling for me
on cold gray morns
I'd be hard an' take her
       till I'd shudder off
she'd make her grumbles
love but hot wax gone cold
then to the Battery I'd walk
suck salt air for a dream
walk back through laborers
the roaring chaos of this city
seeing no love 'cept in the young

VI.   1970 The Modern

I see the ladies in their glory
drinking an' smoking
equals with the lads
they'll be no more farms

no more homes as we knew
hot tea, a crust of bread
the damn damp in here
no woman'll listen to us

On these winged things we fly
hours an' you're back in Ireland
I'm an old ignorant ghost
Cooper himself said we would
just as words ran on wire cable
as iron rails thundered by
no longer so wide this world
lonely 4 a.m. in this bar
I wish a ghost could die

VII.   1986 Changing

Little did I know Will
      loved me in death so
to make a mausoleum here
a boy's fantasy of men an' magic
      as if The Old House At Home
      was of another world, ha!
so I died an' he stayed on
      put in a modern shithouse
urinals of marble, shoulder-high
I would have loved to gone here
where millions have pissed
my favorite spot that wood near
      the handle, beveled
by millions of men's fingers

An' now the pisser for the ladies
the kitchen moved over there
where once Sloan sketched me
an old man sitting at a window

VIII.   2000 A Father's Blight

Ah, Will, little did I know ye
methinks a vision cramped
no ambition, no hopes
what must a father do
      I no longer ask
the blight of County Tyrone
      black p'tatoes, black hope
a pocked curse on this house

I have watched ye run my pub
steer a speakeasy ship true
a good few dollars ye made
      but spent not a dime
enjoyed none of this world
grim so grim son of mine
no love was in that breast
was it because ye were childless
that wife barren as the moon?

Your stepmum, Kitty, she said
I should've made time for ye
Take him, she said, walk him
about this grand New York City
      to the bustling docks
      to bloody abbatoirs
      to theatre high an' low
      Harrigan an' Hart
      the Chinatown dens
      the Greene Street brothels
No, I did none, an' ye hung here
in this pub of gobshite an' doom
a mistake it surely was
to show ye no choice

Now a new Millenium
the bother of it all

this old ghost needs to talk
this barman needs to know
        where did ye go, Will?
where's your ghost now?
where're the others?
O, ghosts of my loved ones
waiting right here, I am

ANNIE McSORLEY

(Honora Henley McSorley, called "Annie," married John McSorley in 1855; they had 5 children, 3 surviving her when she died in 1868.)

I. In Passing

I never entered your pub
not then, but I do now
I see you in the night
fingering photographs
I hear you moan, I hear
your ghostbreath catch
for little ones we lost
the hubub modern crowd
knows nothing of us
I saw Peter and Delia
mute near Astor Place
bitter and unforgiving

Your brass nameplated pew
pricey blasphemy it was
a man of God, my arse
they should have seen you
as little Delia and Will saw you
agog with lust for my nurse
your hands on her thighs
the shuddery moans echoing
Peter by the fireplace chewing
the word *why,* like gristle

Of course Peter went west
he smiles slyly now
the devil's a drunk in him
a baseball player here
an outlaw cowboy there

in Santa Fe he was hanged
a horsethief, a robber
the oldest stray furthest

Though I be dead I watched
Delia change to *Mary*
she vowed never to return
so off to the university
to find her architect man
marry and create her world
Kitty cut them off from you
not her blood, so why care
you made no attempt, John
no effort at all to love us

And my little sons?
James and John, my babies?
taken as angels, not old
enough for ghosts as us
another veil, higher I hope
than these pathetic airs
their babyblue eyes flutter
then that ceaseless staring
what wasteful God is this?

II. A Confession

I will tell you this
in the Tompkins Market
remember Sean the costermonger?
I did lay with him
he called my breasts
his lovely turnips
in my garden grew his shoot
my lovely little Will
not yours, John, not yours
the truth I tell you now
fearful I was then

how God might judge me
what say you now?

Can't hear me?
my stray breath I'll blow
in your pasty ghostface
there, a start I see
it's me, Annie
the costermonger took me
seeded Will
his cock my carrot
wake up, you old sot!
you cuckolded fool!
I'll get Will's ghost
to hear truth yet

PETER McSORLEY

(b.1856; first son of John & Honora. Seen in the "McSorley Nine" photo of 1877, he sold liquor from a storefront, broke an engagement, then disappeared from New York.)

I remember the lumberyard
the leather drivin' wheels
the steam fired saws
chuggin' through me boyhood
Tompkins Market across the street
where Mum would take me an' Will
carrots an' spuds, turnips an' onions
"feelin' is knowin'," the man said
lettin' me run me fingers
o'er the roots an' bulbs
the onions were best
me hand fit o'er it fine
that's when the baseball began
playin' in the 9th Street lot
the city sun sweatin' us boys
the crack o' the bat
me whirlin' arm throwin' strikes
the lads knew I'd be a great one

When Mum took to bed all white
I knew she was to die, but not
knowin' it'd take a year an' more
watchin' an' workin', raisin' Will
all you wanted was your feed
the way you looked at the nurse
we couldn't but hear the sounds
a boy seein' his father pumpin'
the girl, big arse in the air
beatin' me was motto 'nough
　be good or be gone
so I made promise to meself
I'd be gone when I needs be

It was when I found me Kate
      o'er on Greene Street
after I broke our engagement
well, I did go see herself
poxed through the rouge
disease doin' damnation
herself knew she was dyin'
—tell 'em I died a whore's death,
—Kate the whore, that's me!—
her cacklin' was sad an' evil
I wished Godspeed an' walked
an' walked to decide me fate
goin' west an' gone for good

KATE

(Fiancée of Peter McSorley. She ran off with a small-time crook, who got her addicted to opium, then sold her off to a Greene Street brothel owner. Disillusioned, Peter began to drink heavily, and shortly thereafter disappeared from New York. Kate died of the pox.)

Hey! Petey the sot! It's me!
Your sweet Kate, ha!
A ghost is a ghost
You should've seen me
Oozin' sores of the pox
Ah, but you did visit
Scared you, I did.
Didn't care, not me
By then a dream was real
I saw what it all meant
Our Mums dyin' of fever
While in the next room
Fathers stuffin' their meat
In the nearest woman

I learned then of love
To be me, Pretty Kate
Best whore in the house
Though last long I didn't
But I told you the truth
An' I'm tellin' you again
Find love in a bottle
Find it in lust
In money an' mostly
In your mind
Yep, love's a killer

DELIA (a.k.a. MARY) McSORLEY

(b. 1858; d. (?). Only daughter of Honora & John; in 1871 she scratched out her name "Delia" in the family Bible, replacing it with "Mary." About this time her father married Kitty. Mary (Delia) went off to the university, meeting and marrying an architect named McCarthy. She distances herself from the family and the bar.)

I saw mother's ghost last night
her wide sad eyes broke me
I wept and wept for what was
her young death, papa's betrayal
an unhealing wound that bled
into decades and centuries, it's
how hate breeds, staining,
always seeping, which is why I
changed my name back then
when he said he and Kitty were
to marry, I knew I was no more,
so I became *Mary,* née Delia
to forget that sorrow I saw
yet still glows in these ghosts

I found my architect love
a grand life we lived, books,
buildings, family, university,
worlds apart from the bar
but still here in my breast
this bitter sliver from papa
his betrayal for us to hear
while you lay dying, I still
feel your feverish hand
what haunting thing this is
to return after a good life
to have surface this thorn
so deep beyond forgiving

Delia McSorley?
Mary McCarthy?
that nags herself so
what ghost is this?

JAMES McSORLEY

(b. 1860, d. 1861; baby James lived 10 months; second son born to John & Honora McSorley.)

There was no I
in the normal way
not yet, not yet

Only her voice
soothing warm
her touch on me

My mouth on her breast
sucking the wetwhite
warm murmurs

There was him
smoky hot voice
from the wordhole

I could feel my face
creasing a smile
sounds burbling

Then it got hot
things went red
then came black

A slow sleepblack
what is strange is
how no one remembers

Even as this small shade
I move lonely near others
still seeking her touch

BILL McSORLEY

(b. 1861, d. 1938. William McSorley was the third son of John & Honora; he took over the daily running of The Old House At Home after his father died in 1910, leasing the bar from his stepmother, Kitty. He finally owned it outright upon her death in 1928, after buying out Delia's share of the inheritance. In 1936, he sold McSorley's to Daniel O'Connell, a New York City policeman.)

I.   On A Father Dying: 1910

>Now you join Mum in Calvary
>separated by Kitty's plot
>the terrible row over this
>echoes likely in your worm bar
>no doubt our ghosts carry on
>you an' Mum make your peace
>
>Refused to ride horseless I did
>those noisy cars you hated
>so alone I went, the horses
>clipclopping as the sad snow fell
>voices slurring into beery quiet
>I fear I must raise the price

II.   Changes: 1911

>Plumbing done, the big pissers
>installed, urinals they say
>old Joe already fell in
>the new kitchen room aside
>now the hob for specials only
>a nickel for the ales will hold
>
>To your Kitty I swore loyal
>she dislikes me an' all know it

to your memory true I'll run
the house till I die, but herself
she lives only for her Jennie
an' will not turn the pub to me

So 'tis mine an' not mine
the Old House At Home is done
nothing will change, by God
the men pat me on the back
for 'tis your name on the bar
McSorley's Old Ale House

III.   Speakeasy Walls: A Midnight in 1924

Hear me, Father? You do.
I feel you, moving slowly
stirring dust, eyeing pictures
the sun is forbidden now
a steady gaslight in our cave
nothing ever changes, really

All light has been curtained since
the Temperance wankers won
down the hallway the lads come
two taps an' Kelly slides the peep
easy words an' they're in like Flynn
the town is wet an' mad for more

But not to worry, for Lloyd
runs the precinct an' O'Connell
captains the cops, we'll survive
as the ale comes by Buggy's truck
his heartless brewery using yeast
from Butt's Green, so they say

The Great War has come an' gone
lots of regular lads won't be back

Farnan, Curran an' Mahoney
Smith, Lynch, Noone an' Heaney
Bateson, Coyne an' Thornton, an'
all the rest hanging on the gasline
wishbones of the dead growing dust

IV. A Midnight In Summer: 1932

For years I've been Old Bill
a cynic, gloomy an' stingy
but now Kitty's dead, it's mine
love at best a mystery, half
a century now Mum's gone,
Sarah was barren, you dead
all that's left is McSorley's

Where I've kept you alive
amongst addled men talking
politics, dead love, bad jobs
illness an' friends blown to bits
the painter Sloan wrote hello
from New Mexico, wasn't that
where Peter was hanged?

I added an end piece of bar
mahogany curling round
fronting the clipper's ice box
more room for the sotted men
the cats feed out back now
fishheads, milk an' liverscraps

At times I hear Mum moaning
'tis so cold in the black air
in the wee hours I feel her
ashimmer, near the coal stove
her ghost like heat off embers
I ask Mum, *what should I do?*

That eerie May four summers past
her howling an' stomping upstairs
went stark mad at Kitty's corpse
only one she knew for fifty years
like living in a cave, poor girl
I put your Jennie in Creedmore

Al Smith ran for President in '28
Roosevelt's got the chance now
they say Europe's a bog an' we're
as poor as can be, us Irish sods
I move slower as the light fades
my fingers clawed like my soul

V.   Selling Out: 1936

I've done the deed an' sold to
O'Connell who loves this place
a special pub for the men
so he says, a public lair where
wounds get licked, plots hatched
ideas kicked, he goes on an' on

Prohibition gone now, to ban
drink was a fool's game, good
for those ignorant of the heart
now I sit, hunched an' worn
nursing an ale, wondering why
the walls speak in tongues

I keep turning to you
this crazy rage in my craw
I want to grab you, old man
shake the why from you
the reasons for the way 'tis
this silence in your walls

SARAH McSORLEY

(b. 1867; d. 1948; Sarah and Bill McSorley, childless, were married circa 1886.)

I outlived all of you
though no good to me
the stinkin' pub lives on
the men so weak an' vile
stuffin' their heart an' soul
with cheese an' ale
what hope had I?
marryin' you, obsessed
crazed son of himself
I wanted children, too
God's will be done

The pub your real home
the men your family
arselickin' for free drinks
laughin' at inanities
obscene girly jokes
the only decent one Sloan
paintin' real cityfolk
I had eyes for him

But no, I married to flee
only to imprison meself
fear kept me bound
what could a woman do?

Kitty an' meself didn't speak
what was there for words?
weak Jennie was her curse
an' Kitty in truth was ours
God's makin' me pay, she said
Forgive me, I'll only lease to Bill

'cause he hates me so
she told me herself she did
you never could forgive

The old man made you sour
not *me*, barren wordless Sarah
Kitty was right 'bout it
your mother with her curse
on bar an' family alike
I hear their ghosts moanin'
still waitin' for us to talk

JOHN McSORLEY

(b. 1863, d. 1864; baby John lived but 10 months, the fourth and last son of John & Honora McSorley.)

But a smidgen in time
my baby body red an' wet
a kicker I was so kicked

Inside me Mum
I swum an' swum
kickin' me paddles

The rope that was cord
I could grab an' pull
feelin' the tug o' Mum

Then the water went 'way
my head went to light
an' born I got

Cooin' an' yammerin'
I sucked an' shat
'til I grew to smile

Pete's thumb I gripped tight
o'er an' o'er my little fingers
grabbin' for some hold

It was o'er an' done quick
real hot an' real cold
then this rollin' darkness

KITTY McSORLEY

(b. 1846, d. 1928. Katherine Donovan, second wife of John McSorley. "Kitty" was the live-in nurse for the moribund Annie McSorley, John's first wife. She likely provided some sort of childcare for Peter, Delia, and Bill while their mother was still alive. She married John McSorley in 1870 or 1871.)

You being the older man
you knew the mystery
how the world worked
men, money, love, power
who to befriend, who to stab
when to shutup, when to gab
dirty secrets in the pocket
but knowing that world
is but one thing
caring is different
there's no power in it
you give because you love
because you must
Jennie became my life
I offer no apology for it
this was part of God's play

You stopped the drink
yet couldn't break from the bar
your men games, the power
politics, money, women
it was who you were
just as I am what I did
at first I thought I was free
stealing your love from her
how foolish to think I could
steal from you, a barman

A curse of sadness on us
from her deathbed whispers
who believes such things?
then the little ones began
Little JohnJohn crushed
Kitty wheezing for air
Edward too weak to live
runaway Frank wanted
    nothing to do with us
George dying at Rockaway
and Jennie, my poor baby
addled by Annie's curse
the design is hers
tugging on that thread
ravelling our fates

JOHN J. McSORLEY

(b. 1872, d. 1879. First-born son of Kitty & John McSorley. Seven years old when he dies of a crushed skull, run over by the ale delivery wagon. He is the little boy in the picnic photograph on the bar wall.)

Leathery horse balls
smoke off the turds
as they fall in the mud
crack of oak barrels
against one another
one time the bung blew
smell of ale gushing
I remember Mum's leg
holding so tightly
looking up always
into people's mouths
toothstump stench
when they bent down
blowing their words
into my littleboy world

Little JohnJohn, they
yelled at me, stay clear
always hollering to be
away, but I couldn't
loving the horsesmells
legs stomping, nostrils
snorting their warning
as the kegs rolled from
wagon-ramps, how was I
to know when I whipped
the big rump the horse
would rear an' I slip down
where the big wheel came

KATHERINE LORETTA McSORLEY

(b. 1874, d. 1878. First-born daughter of John & Kitty McSorley, she dies of childhood pneumonia less than a year before her brother dies in the wagon accident.)

Buttery bread so warm
my favorite taste
I dress my doll
her name is Dolly
rain tap-tapping glass
trying to touch me
Mum lets me sit here
by the window
crackling snaps the fire
orange, red, yellow
I'm sick cold
it's hard breathing
I see kids at market
Mum says I can go
with her next week
Dolly is dressed now
we are ready for the trip
it just keeps raining
I feel so cold inside
Mum says sit closer
to the fire where it's
warm but I cough
I cough to breathe

EDWARD McSORLEY

(b. 1881, d. 1882. Third son of John & Kitty McSorley. Dies in infancy.)

Sensation was all.
Warm milk from her nipple.
Liquid warmth down my gullet.
Warm piss in my crotch.
A cold in my stools.
Not enough water inside.
I shat everything faster.
And faster.
It didn't take long.
I could see the breast.
But there wasn't strength
In my lips for the suck.

GEORGE McSORLEY

(b. 1883, d. 1906. Last born son of John & Kitty McSorley. He died after breaking his neck in a diving accident at Rockaway Beach.)

A beachcomber I was
my toes sinking in hot sand
my mind swooning for sky
a kite teasing its tether
leashed by the old man
his stinking bar there to
jail dreams, damn his soul
like sawdust everywhere
between blurry draughts
the barhuggers think wisdom
is something peculiar

There was nothing really
to rescue, surely not me
the curse an unseen tattoo
feeling but never knowing
when, with Pete hanging
there in my mind, next to
JohnJohn's crushed skull
the sliver of his bone we
furtively kept as a relic
a totem against the curse
I knew I wouldn't escape
though on that sunblazing
noon at Rockaway
with the hot sand
clinging to my limbs
I dove into the ocean
breaking my neck in
invisible places
which, nonetheless,
had been marked...

JENNIE McSORLEY

(b. 1880, d. 1940. The second daughter of John & Kitty McSorley, Jennie was born with some order of brain dysfunction. She lived in the apartment above the bar with her mother and father. Kitty devoted her life to Jennie's care, and when Kitty died in 1928, Bill McSorley committed Jennie to Creedmore Mental Institution, where she died.)

I heard him say it.
In the past tense.
No longer am I a beauty.
He told the men down there
    with their big nasty things
I was the most beautiful thing.
But addled.
She's aging badly.
Mum said they're really all
    the same, that it's best
I never went out much.
Once the man with the moustache
    grabbed his pants there.
Sticking his tongue at me.
I stuck mine back. Addled.
That raucous laughing of the men.
And Mum so angry with me.
Once when she was bathing
    she held her breasts to me.
    Saying the men wanted them.
But I was fortunate, she said. Never
    would they touch me. Nothing.
    I would miss nothing.

My skin became flour white, whiter
    than drifting clouds.
I watched them from the window.
Then wrinkles came. You see.
I watched my skin.
And the clouds.

Listening for words of the men.
Mum said Little Kitty used to stare
    from this very window.
Years ago. In the last century.
If that was in this world.
Mum tried to explain time to me.

The sky is just skin.
Once. In the market on the Avenue.
The butcherman looked in my eyes
    saying I was his dream.
I asked him what all the red things were.
He was confused. What red things?
Then I swept my pointfinger over all.
    Meat. Just meat, he said.
Next week was when George got dead.
The butcherman showed me the neck.

Father died then. Mum was all
    teary to cry anytime.
We went for the long walks.
Down to the ocean where ships
    came, honking like gulls.
I liked the air smell. A free thing
    by the water. The wind moans.
Sometimes Mum would leave me
    on the bench. A sailorman
    came to see me once.
In his pants he put my hand.
The big nasty thing was there
    to make him happy.
He put his hand on me. My eyes
    closed. I dreamed to float.
On the cloud was the butcherman
    whispering to me.
And the sailorman on my side
    with his touch.
I never told Mum.

So in the morning I woke.
But Mum was still asleep.
Finally I touched her. She was cold.
And very hard. I sat at the window
    and watched a long time.
It was all gray. No clouds came.
Sarah stopped the next morning.
She yelled and yelled. I didn't know
    death had come for Mum.
I got scared and cried a long time.
Mr. Bill said many bad words about
    the addle thing and visits.
I got to ride in the black automobile.
In the gray place with hard steel
    there was only one window.
I never saw a cloud there.
Never ever.
I listened to the radio.
I asked about the clouds.
Did the clouds die? I asked.
I waited for my float dream.